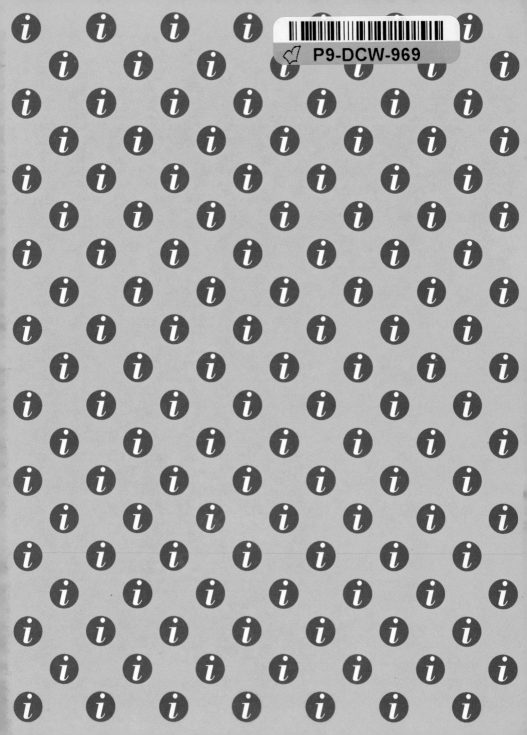

P9-DCW-969

IDENTIFYING
COCA-COLA
COLLECTIBLES

The new compact study guide and identifier

IDENTIFYING

COCA-COLA COLLECTIBLES

The new compact study guide and identifier

Bill Bateman and Randy Schaeffer

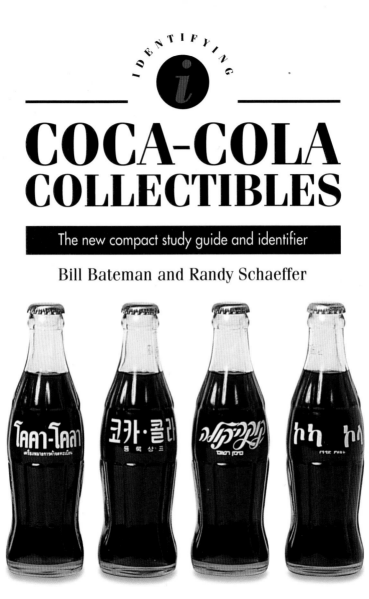

CHARTWELL
BOOKS, INC.

A QUINTET BOOK

Published by Chartwell Books
A Division of Book Sales, Inc.
114 Northfield Avenue
Edison, New Jersey 08837

This edition produced for sale
in the USA, its territories
and dependencies only.

ISBN 0-7858-0773-X

This book was designed and produced by
Quintet Publishing Limited
6 Blundell Street
London N7 9BH

Creative Director: Richard Dewing
Designer: James Lawrence
Senior Editor: Laura Sandelson
Editor: Deborah Gray
Photographer: Ian Howes

Typeset in Great Britain by
Central Southern Typesetters, Eastbourne
Manufactured in Singapore by
Bright Arts Pte Ltd
Printed in China by
Leefung-Asco Printers Ltd

**All of the items shown in this book come from
the William E. Bateman and Randy S. Schaeffer
collection.**

The authors assume full responsibility for facts and
information contained in this book. All opinions
expressed are those of the authors and not of
The Coca-Cola Company.

"Coca-Cola" and "Coke" are registered trademarks which
identify the same product of The Coca-Cola Company.

CONTENTS

ABOVE *Cardboard sign, c. 1925, 8½ x 3½ inches.
Before the popularity of six-bottle cartons, bottlers
used signs such as this one to encourage people to
keep bottles of Coca-Cola on ice at home.*

INTRODUCTION

For more than a century, Coca-Cola has been an integral part of American life. From its humble beginnings in 1886 in Atlanta, Georgia, to its current status as the world's pre-eminent soft drink, Coca-Cola has been heavily advertised using virtually every trick in the adman's repertoire. Long before today's mass media, The Coca-Cola Company used millions of promotional items to advertise and sell their product to the masses. These items ranged from utilitarian merchandising items such as bottles and coolers to traditional and familiar advertising items such as signs and print advertisements; from point-of-purchase items such as trays and calendars to complimentary novelties such as toys and bookmarks.

ABOVE *Cardboard cutout, 1929, 31 inches wide. This sign is the centerpiece of the five-piece "Nasturtium" festoon, which would have been used to decorate the backbar of a soda fountain.*

These items form the basis for today's collections of Coca-Cola memorabilia. Part of the charm of these items for the collector is that their original purpose was to promote the sale of Coca-Cola, not to be collected. Naturally, many of the older items have not survived for today's collectors. Hence, rarity plays a role in the evaluation of Coca-Cola collectibles as does the condition of the material. A third factor used to evaluate Coca-Cola collectibles is the desirability of the items themselves. For example, objects that show pictorial artwork are usually more highly prized than those which do not.

In the area of "antique advertising," Coca-Cola items are regarded as the premier collectibles and invariably command the highest prices.

The articles used to advertise Coca-Cola were usually made of the best-quality materials. For example, it cost The Coca-Cola Company $5,000 just for the dies needed to produce a self-framed metal sign featuring "Betty," the Coca-Cola girl for 1914. The attractiveness of these items also accounts in part for the high survival rate, since many people saved these items at the time. The result for the collector is a rich variety of memorabilia unparalleled by any other consumer product.

LEFT *Cardboard cutout, 1926, 18 inches high. The boy vendor shown in this artwork would have been a familiar sight at ballparks in the 1920s. It was also produced in a nearly life-sized version.*

ABOVE *Metal sign, 1914, 30¾ x 41 inches. One of the largest metal Coca-Cola signs for indoor use, this self-framed sign was made by the Passaic Metal Ware Company. The same "Betty" artwork was used on the trays and calendars for 1914.*

The considerable interest in collecting older items has created a secondary level of new collectible items especially for sale to collectors as well as to the general public. At first The Coca-Cola Company discouraged such efforts, but now through licensing agreements with various manufacturers, the Company helps to identify images and items that may be produced. New items using old artwork fall into two categories: those that closely imitate old items are called reproductions, and those that do not are called fantasy items. Since many of these new things appear older than they actually are, collectors not only have to be knowledgeable about older items, but also about reproduction and fantasy items.

As The Coca-Cola Company expanded its activities to more than 195 countries around the world, they have individualized the advertising approach to the countries in which Coca-Cola is sold. Not only are the many languages distinctive, but the pieces themselves are often unique to a specific country. Such items are especially prized when the artwork reflects the culture of the native country, rather than merely being an imitation of advertising used in the United States. No matter what country they hail

ABOVE *Paper poster, 1947, 16 x 27 inches. Although this sign was printed in the United States, the language is Dutch, indicating that it was meant for export to the Netherlands.*

from, most Coca-Cola collectors eagerly add foreign Coca-Cola items to their collections when they have the opportunity.

Although it has become an international product, Coca-Cola is regarded worldwide as the quintessential icon of American life. Coca-Cola collectibles hold a mirror to America's past and present: its customs, values, tastes, obsessions, pleasures, and troubles. For many people, collecting the advertising in use when they were growing up allows them to recapture simpler times. For others, the advertising of Coca-Cola exemplifies the dream of a better way of life.

ABOVE *Cardboard sign, 1933, 10¼ x 19¾ inches. During the 1930s, signs such as this one were used to promote drinking Coca-Cola at mealtimes. Called a hanger, this sign is die-cut and folded, giving it a three-dimensional effect.*

A BRIEF HISTORY

Dr John S. Pemberton is said to have first concocted Coca-Cola in the spring of 1886. Prior to that time, he had marketed many different products, one of which was called "French Wine Coca," because of its two main components, Bordeaux wine and extract of cocoa. By 1886, in an effort to get on the anti-alcohol temperance bandwagon, Pemberton decided to make a non-alcoholic product based on French Wine Coca by

ABOVE *Spoon, c. 1895, 6 inches long. With its embossed bowl, this silver-plated spoon was used to mix the finished product in a glass after Coca-Cola syrup and carbonated water had been added individually.*

ABOVE *Paper label, 1885, 2 x 3⅞ inches. In addition to coca and wine, Pemberton's French Wine Coca also contained kola nut extract, recognized as a headache cure and hangover remedy because of its caffeine content. Bottles of the product were packaged in boxes with this label.*

eliminating the wine. To help mask the relatively unpleasant taste of this mixture of coca and kola, he added several aromatic oils and spices: lemon, orange, vanilla, nutmeg, coriander, cinnamon, etc. The resultant product was then sold as an over-the-counter medicine to be taken "a teaspoonful in a glass of water."

By 1887, Pemberton apparently had decided that carbonated water was the mixer to use.

Pemberton began selling his interest in Coca-Cola during the summer of 1887. Asa G. Candler, a fellow druggist, was interested in Coca-Cola because he had tried it for his persistent headaches and "was relieved," not once, but on several occasions. As a druggist, Candler would have found headache relief significant since the pain-relieving properties of aspirin were not discovered until a dozen years later.

Through a series of transactions, Candler gained total control of Coca-Cola

BELOW *Free-drink coupon, letter, and envelope, c. 1895. As a means of promoting Coca-Cola, the Company mailed coupons for free drinks to potential customers from lists supplied by local soda fountain operators.*

ABOVE *Photograph, 1909, 7⅝ x 9½ inches. Taken at the 1909 New Jersey Fair, this photograph shows the award-winning Coca-Cola booth. Close examination reveals dozens of Coca-Cola advertising items including signs, trays, posters, cutouts, bottles, openers, glasses, 24-bottle cases, fans, and thermometers.*

by the end of the summer of 1888 for an investment of just over $2,300. On April 13, 1891, Candler became the "sole proprietor" of Coca-Cola and incorporated the business the following year. Pre-1890 items available to collectors are letters written by Pemberton, Candler, and others on stationery imprinted with "Coca-Cola."

From its very beginning, Coca-Cola was advertising heavily. The philosophy for this marketing approach appears in 1892. Candler stated: "We have done very considerable advertising in territory which has not yet yielded any returns. We have reason to believe that it will show good returns during the ensuing year."

Pre-1900 Coca-Cola collectibles include stationery, booklets, postcards, trade cards, free-drink coupons, calendars, bookmarks, trays, clocks, syrup urns, fans, napkins, canvas banners, paper and cardboard posters, and metal signs.

BELOW *Letterhead, 1907, 8⅜ inches wide. After starting in Atlanta, The Coca-Cola Company soon had branches scattered throughout the United States, Canada, and Cuba, as shown on this elaborate letterhead.*

ABOVE *Ceramic syrup urn, c. 1900, 18 inches high. The upper portion of this three-piece unit held approximately one gallon of Coca-Cola syrup. A spigot on the reverse side (not visible in photo) was used to dispense the syrup directly into a glass.*

RIGHT *Cardboard fan, c. 1893, 8½ x 12⅛ inches. This fan is just one of many examples of local advertising for Coca-Cola.*

LEFT *Cardboard streetcar sign, 1918, 21 x 11 inches. In an obvious appeal to patriotism, this sign shows the silhouette of the Statue of Liberty's torch as the shadow of a hand holding a glass of Coca-Cola.*

BELOW *Trade card, c. 1907, 6¼ x 3½ inches folded (closed, open, and rear views shown). This amusing metamorphic "Bathtub" trade card opens to reveal that the woman's knees are actually the heads of men being served Coca-Cola.*

The decade from 1901 to 1910 saw a continued increase in sales from 1,300 to 11,500 gallons a day and an increase from $100,000 spent on advertising in 1901 to $850,000 in 1910. Coca-Cola was first advertised in national consumer magazines in the summer of 1904, although previously there had been advertising in some drug and religious publications.

The independently owned bottling business also thrived, and by the end of the decade in 1910, local bottlers were using over 30% of all the syrup produced. Increasingly, advertising depicted Coca-Cola in bottles, and the use of advertising novelties increased exponentially.

Sales of Coca-Cola steadily increased in volume from 1886 to 1917. In 1917, however, the United States found itself involved in World War I. Many staples were rationed, most notably sugar, one of the two main ingredients of Coca-Cola (the other being water). These conditions forced the Company to curtail the production of syrup.

The years following the war were unsettled ones for Coca-Cola. The price of sugar continued to fluctuate and a trademark infringement case with the Koke Company initiated back in 1912 remained unsettled. These uncertainties led to the sale of the company to a consortium of banks; consequently, Coca-Cola became a publicly held company registered in Delaware.

In 1920 the legal case against Koke was settled in Coca-Cola's favor and an energetic new management was established. The advertising strategy once more became dynamic and sales rebounded.

Two merchandising firsts occurred in the 1920s: the first six-bottle carton in 1923 and the first standardized cooler for bottled Coca-Cola in 1929. Two new advertising media were added during the decade: 24-sheet billboards and radio programs. Many of the famous slogans associated with Coca-Cola also had their beginnings in the 1920s: "Thirst knows no season," "Enjoy thirst," and "Refresh yourself." By 1928, the sales of bottled Coca-Cola surpassed forever the fountain sales of Coca-Cola.

ABOVE RIGHT *Magazine advertisement, 1922, 10 x 13¾ inches. Prior to World War I, soft drinks were thought of and advertised as being primarily summertime drinks. In the 1920s, the Company began vigorously promoting Coca-Cola as the drink that "knows no season."*

ABOVE LEFT *Cardboard cutout, 1924, 40 inches high. During the first few decades of the century, the Company used the same "Coca-Cola Girl" on a variety of advertising items for a particular year. The girl shown here was also used on trays and calendars in 1924.*

The decade of the 1930s was marked by continued growth for The Coca-Cola Company. Coca-Cola continued to thrive during the Great Depression, while other soft drinks and businesses failed. That this was also the Golden Age of Hollywood was not lost on those in charge of the advertising for Coca-Cola. Numerous movie stars were shown, always with conspicuously present bottles and glasses of Coca-Cola, as if to say that drinking Coca-Cola would make the common person's life more glamorous. The cavalcade of stars used on Coca-Cola advertising included many of filmdom's finest, for instance, Joan Blondell, Claudette Colbert, Jackie Cooper, Joan Crawford, Clark Gable, Cary Grant, Jean Harlow, and Maureen O'Sullivan. Cardboard signs, cutouts, and posters showing these stars are extremely popular with today's collectors.

ABOVE *Cardboard cutout, 1933, 63 inches high. Shown here on a fountain stool and in more conventional dress, Maureen O'Sullivan is perhaps best known for playing "Jane" to Johnny Weissmuller's "Tarzan" in the movies.*

LEFT *Price lists, for 1938 and 1939, 11 x 15 inches closed. The Coca-Cola Company offered standardized advertising materials to the bottlers through these annual price lists.*

SERVICE ABOVE SELF

Be a Lifesaver — Buy War Bonds and Stamps

Armed only with courage, and dedicated to saving life and relieving pain, the men of the Medical Department go into battle. Where shells scream and bullets whine these men perform their duty. A minute saved may mean a life saved. Beside the men who fall they serve, giving first aid, quenching thirst, guarding until stretchers come. Theirs is a true devotion to mercy, a Service Above Self!

1943   October   1943

SUNDAY	MONDAY	TUESDAY	WEDNESDAY	THURSDAY	FRIDAY	SATURDAY
					1	2
3	4	5	6	7	8	9
10	11	12	13	14	15	16
17	18	19	20	21	22	23
24 31	25	26	27	28	29	30

DELICIOUS *Coca-Cola* REFRESHING

THE COCA-COLA BOTTLING WORKS COMPANY

ABOVE *Wooden sign, 1934, 15 x 20 inches. The National Recovery Administration (NRA) was established in 1933 by President Franklin D. Roosevelt to regulate industry and labor practices.*

LEFT *Calendar, 1943, 19 x 39½ inches. Through a project called "Schools at War," Coca-Cola bottlers distributed this calendar to encourage children to save their dimes for the war effort.*

RIGHT *Cardboard cutout display, 1933, 43¼ inches wide. The Coca-Cola Company commissioned Ida Bailey Allen, a recognized expert on food and nutrition, to write "When You Entertain," a small book containing hospitality hints.*

Naturally, the decade of the 1940s was dominated by World War II. Company President Woodruff set the tone for the operating procedure when he directed that, "We will see that every man in uniform gets a bottle of Coca-Cola for five cents wherever he is and whatever it costs." The Company carried out this pledge by building bottling plants overseas as near to the troops as possible.

The war was the predominant advertising theme during this time period. Countless posters, signs, cardboard cutouts, and calendars portrayed both men and women in uniform.

In 1941, the Company officially started using the nickname "Coke" as a synonymous name for Coca-Cola. "Coke" was finally registered as a trademark in the United States Patent Office on August 14, 1945.

ABOVE *Plastic bottle topper, 1953, 7 x 7¼ inches. Although the Company had long fought against using nicknames for Coca-Cola, they finally relented and adopted the trademark "Coke" in the 1940s. When placed atop an ordinary bottle, this display piece reminded the public that they could use either name to get the same drink.*

LEFT AND BELOW *Playing cards, 1943. By showing silhouettes of Allied and Axis planes, this deck of "Spotter Cards" was meant to help servicemen abroad, as well as citizens at home, identify military aircraft. The woman on the reverse side is a U.S. Army Nurse.*

ABOVE *Metal sign, 1968, 11¾ x 18 inches. Since the 1950s, the Company has also made a line of fruit-flavored soft drinks called Fanta.*

During the 1950s new bottle sizes, vending machines and flat-topped cans were introduced. The Coca-Cola Company departed from its one-product rule with the introduction of the Fanta line of flavors. Sprite, TAB, Fresca, and Simba followed in the 1960s.

Advertising for Coca-Cola entered the television era with the sponsorship of ventriloquist Edgar Bergan, Walt Disney and Kit Carson. Later in the 1960s Coca-Cola took on a "hip" image as popular singers such as the Supremes, Ray Charles, and Aretha Franklin were recruited to promote Coca-Cola.

A new slogan and logo made a grand entrance in 1969. The slogan was "It's the real thing" and the logo was called "Arden Square" with the "dynamic ribbon device" appearing below the trademark.

ABOVE *Cardboard cutout, c. 1953, 13¼ inches high. Western frontiersman Kit Carson, as portrayed by actor Bill Williams, was immortalized in a 1950s television series sponsored by local Coca-Cola bottlers.*

ABOVE *Paper flyer, 1965, 11¾ x 8 inches. Many popular artists were used to advertise Coca-Cola, but not the Beatles. However, a bottler in Cleveland, Ohio, did sponsor a program about them on a local television station.*

ABOVE   *Can, 1985, 5¾ inches high. At a development cost of approximately $250,000, The Coca-Cola Company produced about 300 "Space Cans," several of which went into space aboard the Challenger Space Shuttle. On July 31, 1985, Coca-Cola became the first carbonated soda to be drunk in space.*

Since that time, there have been other milestones in the history of The Coca-Cola Company, but with little impact on Coca-Cola collecting. The 1971 commercial song "I'd like to teach the world to sing . . ." broke into the charts, selling well over a million copies.

The 1980s spawned the creation of "megabrand" Coca-Cola comprising diet Coke, caffeine-free Coke, Cherry Coke, "new" Coke, and Classic Coca-Cola. Coca-Cola also reached another kind of high in 1985 when specially designed cans went aloft in the Space Shuttle, and Coke became the first soft drink to be drunk in space. Back on earth, space-age cans made of plastic were test-marketed by us earthbound mortals in late 1985.

Coca-Cola celebrated its hundredth anniversary in 1986. Since then, The Coca-Cola Company has continued to prosper, and so has collecting Coca-Cola memorabilia.

BELOW   *Paper poster, 1986, 19 x 27¼ inches. The Coca-Cola Company celebrated the 100th anniversary of Coca-Cola during the week of May 8, 1986. The special logo for the Coca-Cola's Centennial Celebration in Atlanta is shown at the bottom of this poster.*

USING THIS GUIDE

This guide provides examples of the major facets of Coca-Cola memorabilia with a brief introduction to the history of The Company. Within each chapter major changes in the design and materials used by Coca-Cola are discussed to help you identify and roughly date memorabilia that you might discover in attics, auctions and flea markets. The 1970s saw an upsurge in interest in vintage Coca-Cola memorabilia, however, it also resulted in an increase in the wholesale manufacture of unlicensed collectibles. As these bogus items themselves age, the more difficult it becomes to identify them as fakes. A knowledgeable collector will be able to detect differences between the original and the reproduction. For example, today's printing processes are different from those used at the turn of the century resulting in subtle differences in size, color, and materials. Apart from the items shown in the last chapter, all the memorabilia illustrated in this guide are photographed from the originals.

There are a few strategies that help the collector identify reproduction materials. First of all, see as many of the original items as possible. Visit antique advertising shows, auctions, and museums. These are good places to meet other collectors and arrange to study their collections. Secondly, increase your knowledge by reading as much as you can. You could begin by concentrating your collection in one area and really getting to know your chosen subject – then you can be sure that you are collecting "the real thing."

BOTTLES

In the early days John Pemberton, who invented Coca-Cola in 1886, used plain bottles with paper labels marked "Coca-Cola Syrup and Extract" to distribute the syrup to soda fountains. At fountains the syrup was mixed with plain water and served to customers. Then in 1894 the carbonated beverage was put in bottles so that people could enjoy the soft drink away from soda fountains.

The first bottles to contain carbonated Coca-Cola were Biedenharn's soda water bottles marked "Biedenharn Candy Co., Vicksburg, Miss.," bottles that he had used previously for other beverages. These thick-walled, six-ounce bottles used Hutchinson stoppers and were not marked with the Coca-Cola trademark.

Asa Candler, president of The Coca-Cola Company, gave two lawyers,

Thomas and Whitehead exclusive rights to bottle Coca-Cola in the entire United States except for the territories covered by pre-existing contracts. Their first bottles marked "Coca-Cola" were Hutchinson-stopper bottles but the use of these bottles for Coca-Cola was short-lived since within two years the more dependable and cheaper crown-top bottles became the industry standard.

1. Syrup bottle, c. 1905, 12 inches high. Kept on the backbars of soda fountains, syrup bottles were used to store small quantities of Coca-Cola syrup until needed.

2. Hutchinson-stopper bottle, c. 1902, 6¼ inches high. To open such a bottle, one had to push down on the wire loop, an action that produced a loud popping sound – the origin of the term "soda pop."

1

2

B OT T L E S : CROWN-TOP BOTTLES

Bottlers soon switched over to the new crown-top bottles. Bottles were hand-blown, glass was mixed in relatively small batches, and bottle sizes were not standardized. The result for today's collectors is a seemingly endless variety of bottles in different shapes, colors, and sizes, with previously unknown bottles still surfacing today. However, collectors generally separate early bottles into two main categories: amber bottles, ranging in color from dark brown to the color of honey; and more transparent bottles including green, blue, aqua, and colorless.

1a and **1b** Bottles with paper labels, c. 1910, clear, 7¼ inches high, and amber, 7½ inches high. Shown here are typical examples of the two colors of bottles used from 1905 to about 1920. Some bottlers thought darker bottles preserved the flavor of Coca-Cola better than lighter bottles.

1a

1b

BOTTLES

These early crown-top bottles were identified as containing Coca-Cola by at least one of the following three devices: (1) the trademark "Coca-Cola" was blown into the glass; (2) the bottle cap was marked with the trademark; and (3) a diamond-shaped paper label printed with the trademark was glued to the side of the bottle. At least nine different versions of authentic paper labels have survived, but they have also been heavily reproduced so that today's collectors often need to consult experts to tell the difference. Bottles first appeared on standard artwork advertising Coca-Cola in 1903 and were clear straight-sided bottles with diamond-shaped paper labels.

1a   **1b**   **1c**   **2**

1a, 1b, and **1c** Bottles, 1920–1950, each 7¾ inches high. The bottles used for all soft drinks were called "flavor bottles" and usually carried the bottler's name with Coca-Cola in block letters, instead of script.

2. Bottle, 1967, 7¾ inches high. When Coca-Cola bottlers began marketing "no-deposit" bottles – ones that were not meant to be returned to the bottler – in the late 1960s, they again turned to straight-sided bottles with paper labels.

BOTTLES

The Coca-Cola Company addressed the need for a standardized bottle for Coca-Cola, mainly to fight the growing problem of imitators. The final design derived its inspiration from a line drawing of a cocoa pod (which had been mistaken for a coca bean), and was patented November 16, 1915. The glass color selected was known as "German green" at the time, but now

called "Georgia Green" in honor of the home state of Coca-Cola. The prototype bottle, which had an exaggerated bulge around the middle, was then modified to fit automatic bottling equipment.

By 1920s, the new standardized bottle – called a hobbleskirt bottle because its shape resembled a dress fashion of the day – was in widespread use throughout the United States.

1. Bottles, 1986, each 7½ inches high. As the world's most recognized container, the hobbleskirt bottle has been produced for international use. Shown here from left to right are bottles from China, Bulgaria, Morocco, Japan, United States, Thailand, Korea, Israel, and Ethiopia.

2. Cardboard cutout, 1937, 44⅛ inches high, showing the hobbleskirt bottle.

3. Wooden carrier, c. 1926, 8⅛ x 5½ x 5 inches. With dove-tailed corners and rope handle, this finely crafted carrier was one of the earliest forerunners of the cardboard six-pack carton.

BOTTLES: Cans, Cases, and Cartons

Coca-Cola was first packaged in flat-top cans in 1955, but on a limited basis for overseas American military personnel. The late 1960s and early 1970s saw the first widespread use of non-returnable bottles, first made of glass and later plastic.

Cases, cartons, and carriers are also associated with collecting bottles. At first, bottles of Coca-Cola were transported in traditional 24-bottle wooden cases stenciled with the trademark "Coca-Cola." Since 24 bottles were too many for the average consumer at one time, the Company introduced the six-bottle cardboard carton in the mid-1920s. Because of a lack of standardization for cases, cartons, and carriers, there are countless examples for today's collectors.

1. Can, 1956, 4⅞ inches high. The first flat-topped cans for Coca-Cola were prepared for shipment to American servicemen in the Pacific and Europe.

2. Can, 1980, 4⅞ inches high. Although Coca-Cola was not sold in the Soviet Union in 1980, the Company arranged to supply the Olympic Village with Coca-Cola for the Moscow Olympics. The cans were never shipped because of President Carter's decision to withdraw the United States team from competition.

3. Can, 1994, 4⅞ inches high. Since the late 1960s, most Coca-Cola cans have been made of aluminum and steel. Ironically, one of the most recent versions features the classic hobbleskirt bottle in its design.

GLASSES: STRAIGHT-SIDED GLASSES

Few people realize that long before that bottle came into existence, the "Coca-Cola glass" had achieved equal recognition. Until the late 1920s, the sale of fountain Coca-Cola (in glasses) far outpaced the sale of Coca-Cola in bottles. Since Coca-Cola was first concocted in 1886, most of it had been served in glasses made specially for Coca-Cola. Consumers had come to associate the product with the glass and the glass with the product.

In 1900 the Company began promoting a "graduated Coca-Cola glass." This "mineral water" glass was a straight-sided glass to which the script Coca-Cola trademark had been added. The word "graduated" referred to the line on the glass approximately three-quarters of an inch from the bottom –

this line was very important because it indicated the amount of Coca-Cola syrup to be used.

The Company soon introduced a metal holder marked "Coca-Cola" specially made to hold straight-sided glasses. Collectors should be aware that The Coca-Cola Company reproduced the metal holder in the 1970s.

1. Straight-sided glass and metal holder, c. 1902, 4¼ inches high. Straight-sided glasses in nickel silver holders appeared in Coca-Cola advertising from 1901 through 1904.

1

GLASSES: FLARE GLASSES

In 1905, the Company introduced the "flare" or "bell" glass. This glass became a sight so familiar throughout the world for the next two decades that the very shape of the glass was instantly associated with Coca-Cola.

In 1923, the Company introduced a new glass with a turned edge at the rim.

Called a "modified flare glass" by today's collectors, this glass was widely touted at Company functions as the perfect glass for Coca-Cola. By 1926, four million modified flare glasses had been sold for fountain use. The Coca-Cola glass underwent another significant change in 1929 when the turned edge

at the top was made even more pronounced, giving the glass a distinct bulge about half an inch from the top. The glass industry called this a "cupped" glass, but today's collectors, somewhat ironically, call it a "bell" glass.

1a

1b

1c

1a, 1b and **1c** Flare glass, c. 1910; large 5¢ glass, 1912, and small 5¢ glass, 1913, each approximately 4 inches high. Shown here are three examples of the flare glasses that were in common use in soda fountains from 1905 to the early 1920s.

2. Modified flare glass, c. 1925, 3¾ inches high. Because the rim of a flare glass was so easily chipped when knocked over, Coca-Cola glasses were slightly modified in 1923 to alleviate this problem.

2

GLASSES

Thus, by 1930 the evolution in the shape of the Coca-Cola glass had ended. In the spring of 1955, The Coca-Cola Company began test-marketing twelve-ounce glasses followed in 1961 by a sixteen-ounce "Jumbo" to accommodate a scoop of ice cream for the "Float with Coke" campaign.

Since the 1960s, fountain glasses for Coca-Cola have undergone countless major changes. Although bell-shaped glasses are still available in a variety of sizes, other shapes, often with colorful printing portraying cartoon characters or traditional Coca-Cola artwork, are extensively used, especially as part of promotions at fast-food outlets.

1. Bell-shaped glass, 1936, 4 inches high. Every person at The Coca-Cola Fountain Sales Corporation's Fiftieth Anniversary Dinner was presented with a personalized bell-shaped glass.

2. Straight-sided glass, 1958, 5⅛ inches high. Non-standard Coca-Cola glasses have been issued periodically to note special occasions.

GLASSES: FOUNTAIN ITEMS

Fountain dispensing machines marked "Coca-Cola" and "Coke" from all periods are also popular collector's items today. However, few collectors have them in working order because the mechanisms needed to make them function properly are both bulky and hard to maintain.

Napkins, coasters, and straws marked Coca-Cola – often used in conjunction with Coca-Cola glasses – are also collected. Amazingly, some pre-1900 tissue paper napkins imprinted with Coca-Cola slogans have survived. There are even straws marked "Coca-Cola." The variety, colorfulness, and availability of such items enhance them as collectibles.

2a

1

2b

2c

1. Box of straws, 1957, 8⅝ inches high. Although this box of 250 straws shows a paper cup, straws were also used with glasses and bottles of Coca-Cola.

2a, 2b, and **2c** Paper cups, c. 1950, 1957, and 1961, each approximately 3¾ inches high. Coca-Cola cups were first introduced in 1941, but did not achieve widespread use until after World War II.

TRAYS AND PLATES

Perhaps no other form of the vast array of items that have been used to advertise Coca-Cola over the years is as closely associated with the product as the "Coca-Cola tray." Beginning in the 1890s and continuing to this day, a series of metal trays has carried forth the "Drink Coca-Cola" message. The enduring qualities of metal, combined with the relatively large number that were produced, have guaranteed the survival of many trays for today's collectors.

1

1. Metal tray, c. 1950, 12¼-inch diameter. Made in London, this British tray might have been used to serve drinks at pubs and restaurants.

2. Metal tray, 1909, 10¼ x 13 inches. Called the "Exposition Girl" artwork, the scene in the background on this tray is typical of world's fairs of the Victorian era.

2

3. Metal tray, 1903, 9¾-inch diameter. The "Bottle Tray" is one of the earliest advertising items to depict the then new straight-sided, paper-label bottle for Coca-Cola.

3

TRAYS AND PLATES

The earliest known tray featuring Coca-Cola dates from 1897. There is an interesting progression in the shape of American Coca-Cola trays, starting with all round trays before 1903, followed by a mixture of round, oval, and rectangular trays from 1921 on. The series ended with the production of the so-called Pansy trays in the 1960s. After that time, The Coca-Cola Company and others began issuing reproduction trays in many shapes.

Although a few examples of Coca-Cola trays were produced for foreign markets as early as the 1920s, most foreign Coca-Cola trays date from after World War II.

1. Metal tray, 1934, 13¼ x 10½ inches. Former Olympic swimming champion Johnny Weissmuller and actress Maureen O'Sullivan are shown on this tray.

2. Metal tray, 1959, 13¼-inch diameter. This tray is typical of a series of round Mexican trays showing Latin women engaged in a variety of activities.

3. Metal plate, c. 1908, 9⅞-inch diameter, in frame, 16 x 16 inches. Imitating a fine porcelain portrait plate, this mass-produced metal "Vienna Art" plate, with its ornate frame and shadow box, was distributed to better customers.

1

2

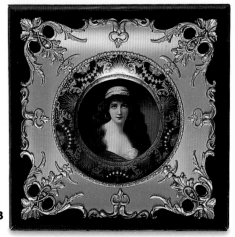

3

TRAYS AND PLATES

Ceramic and glass change receivers were used to advertise Coca-Cola. Larger than a metal change tray, a change receiver was usually located near the cash register. Early examples actually carry the words "Change Receiver" and are quite rare.

In the 1920s, the Company began advertising Coca-Cola as being good with food, consequently, they produced sandwich plates and other china depicting the Coca-Cola bottle and glass. Ceramic, glass, Bakelite, metal, and plastic ashtrays carrying the familiar Coca-Cola logo were also found at many locations where beverages were sold.

2. Glass change receiver, 1911, 7-inch diameter. The advertising message on this change receiver is an example of reverse painting on glass.

1

1. Ceramic plate, 1930, 8¼-inch diameter. The Crockery City Ice & Products Company, the local bottler in East Liverpool, Ohio, arranged to have sandwich plates such as this one made and distributed to other bottlers throughout the country.

3. Ceramic ashtray, c. 1950, 7½ x 7½ inches. Baseball and Coca-Cola, long-standing "partners," were united once again in the advertising on this ashtray.

2

3

COOLERS AND VENDING MACHINES

When the sale of Coca-Cola in bottles first began around the turn of the century, it was the responsibility of the retailer (often a grocer) to see that the bottles were kept chilled. It didn't take long for the bottler to figure out that if he supplied the grocer with a cooler just for Coca-Cola, then an ample supply of properly chilled bottles would always be available for thirsty customers. The first coolers made especially for bottled Coca-Cola were barrels that had been cut in half to form tubs.

Later, more successful wet coolers which were nothing more than wooden boxes on legs were introduced. A sliding or hinged lid along with a metal lining completed the design. More often than not, the outer wooden case was painted with what later became called "Coca-Cola yellow," with stenciled advertising in "Coca-Cola red."

1. Salesman's sample cooler, 1929, 10½ x 7¼ x 13¼ inches. Because Coca-Cola coolers were sold, not given, to retailers, Coca-Cola salesmen were furnished with this miniature version of the standard Glascock cooler so that they could demonstrate its features without having to transport the full-sized model along with them.

COOLERS AND VENDING MACHINES

The next advance in cooler manufacturing in the mid-1920s replaced the wooden exterior with one made of sheet metal. The interior still consisted of a tub filled with ice water to cool the bottles. Additional design features included mechanisms that required customers to insert a warm bottle of soda in order to remove a cold bottle and coin-operated mechanisms that permitted the customer to get only one bottle of soda for a nickel.

In 1945, the Company introduced a new streamlined cooler which featured a completely enclosed base concealing the electric refrigeration unit which by now had become standard. This cooler was the model for the late 1940s cooler-shaped radio and music boxes.

1. Miniature cooler, 1956, 6 x 5 x 8⅞ inches. Handmade from a single block of wood, this miniature is a faithful reproduction of the white-faced cooler, used in the late 1950s.

2. Cooler savings bank, c. 1940, 3⅛ x 4¼ x 1 inches. This bank was given to retailers so that they could save the twenty dollars needed to buy their own coolers.

3. Salesman's sample cooler, 1939, 12⅛ x 7¼ x 10⅛ inches. Although the Coca-Cola cooler was redesigned in 1934, it was not until 1939 that a salesman's sample was produced as part of the "Business Builders" cooler sales contest in that year.

COOLER BOXES AND VENDING MACHINES

The late 1940s and early 1950s marked the change from horizontal coolers to vertical vending machines. Now a machine did more than just cool the bottles; it handled the entire financial transaction, including making change.

Taken as a group, the vending machines produced after 1950 form a bewildering array of shapes, uses, and manufacturers. Many collectors have at least one working cooler or vending machine. Sales items such as miniature salesman samples, brochures, booklets, and assorted novelties are highly prized.

1

2

1. Paper folder, 1941, 9¼ x 12¼ inches. This folder, die-cut in the shape of the 1941 Coca-Cola cooler, was used to advertise the coin-controlled mechanism made by the Vendo Company of Kansas City, Missouri.

2. Vending machine, 1951, 24¼ x 24½ x 64½ inches. Upright vending machines for Coca-Cola were introduced shortly before World War II. This post-war model was called a "C-51" because it was made by the Cavalier Corporation and vended fifty-one bottles.

PERIODICAL ADVERTISING

Advertisements in newspapers and magazines constituted the earliest form of mass media used to advertise Coca-Cola. Because advertising and articles in periodicals have been produced regularly from Coca-Cola's beginnings, they are a rich source not only of collectibles, but also of information about Coca-Cola. Collectors are only beginning to realize the value of collecting such advertising. Collectors must be cautious, however. With the advent of color copiers, unscrupulous individuals have produced photocopies that are difficult to discern from originals.

Coca-Cola was first advertised in *The Daily Journal* newspaper in Atlanta on May 29, 1886. The first known use of script Coca-Cola appeared in *The Daily Journal* on June 16, 1887.

1

1. Magazine advertisement, 1914, 21½ x 15⅛ inches. In a series of magazine ads in the 1910s, the back-cover advertisement for Coca-Cola incorporated the same artwork that was shown on the magazine's front cover.

2

2. Magazine advertisement, 1902, 11 x 8¼ inches. Because drug stores and pharmacies at the turn of the century typically had soda fountain counters, the Company advertised in trade publications such as *The Pharmaceutical Era.*

PERIODICAL ADVERTISING

Beginning in the 1890s, Coca-Cola was heavily promoted in trade publications published for owners and employees of drug stores and soda fountains. These advertisements often explained how much profit could be made by selling Coca-Cola. In addition, these publications occasionally carried articles about Coca-Cola itself.

The Coca-Cola Company first placed advertisements in national consumer magazines in 1904. The same black-and-white ad was placed in six nationally distributed magazines. The Coca-Cola Company and local bottlers began to advertise aggressively in local publications such as telephone directories, high school annuals, church bulletins, and programs for theaters and athletic events. The Coca-Cola Company also published periodicals and one-time publications for the general public. Household entertaining and decorating hints were featured in such publications as the When You Entertain book, and the Pause for Living booklets.

1. Magazine advertisement, 1933, 13½ x 10½ inches. The entire cast of the motion picture *Dinner at Eight* (including Jean Harlow and Lionel Barrymore) was featured in this September 30, 1933, ad in *Saturday Evening Post.*

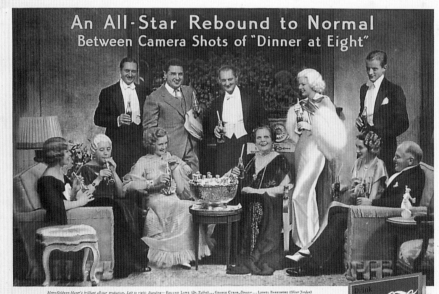

1

PERIODICAL ADVERTISING

1. Newspaper advertisement, 1908, 15½ x 21 inches. Because of the cost involved, it was very unusual for Coca-Cola to be advertised in full-page color newspaper advertisements such as this example from the *Sunday American Examiner.*

2. Baseball program, 1930, 7 x 10⅞ inches. In keeping with its long-standing association with baseball, Coca-Cola was frequently advertised in baseball programs such as this one from Baltimore.

3. Magazine advertisement, 1957, 10¼ x 13½ inches. Shown here is one of a short-lived series of advertisements with stylized artwork showing people enjoying Coca-Cola at locations throughout the world.

1

4. Magazine advertisement, 1920, 8 x 11¼ inches. One of the most beloved magazine advertising campaigns for Coca-Cola in the 1920s used cartoon drawings to portray small-town life such as that shown in this corner pharmacy scene.

2

3

4

CALENDARS

The earliest known Coca-Cola calendar dates from 1891, and the Company has issued annual calendars from that point on. Starting in the mid-1890s, the artwork used on the Coca-Cola calendar was also used on other advertising issued the same year.

In 1904, the Company and parent bottlers began issuing different calendars each year, one for fountain sales and the other for the sale of Coca-Cola in bottles. In most instances, the very same artwork was used, but one version showed a glass of Coca-Cola, while the other showed a bottle. In some years, entirely different artwork was used for the two versions.

1. Calendar, 1908, 7 x 14⅛ inches. The note on the table reads "Good to the Last Drop," a slogan that was later adopted and trademarked by Maxwell House Coffee.

1

38

CALENDARS

1

2

3

1. Calendar, 1911, 10¼ x 18 inches. With artwork copyrighted in 1909, this is one of several Coca-Cola calendars created by the American illustrator Hamilton King, whose signature appears on the calendar.

2. Calendar, 1897, 7½ x 13 inches. The artwork on this calendar has been dubbed the "Victorian Girl."

3. Calendar, 1904, 8¼ x 15¼ inches. Breaking an unwritten rule of not advertising using children, this calendar portraying a child holding a bottle of Coca-Cola was unusual for its day.

CALENDARS

1. Calendar, 1916, 8 x 15 inches. Appearing in an insert in the Sunday edition of the *New York World* newspaper, this summer calendar shows only three months. The model is actress Pearl White, famous for her role in the silent-movie serial *The Perils of Pauline*.

2. Calendar, 1918, 13 x 31⅛ inches. Because of sugar shortages during World War I which reduced production, The Coca-Cola Company advertised very little during 1918. Although Coca-Cola calendars before and after this one were produced in two versions, bottle and glass, only this version was produced in 1918.

CALENDARS

The annual calendars up to 1940 in the United States consisted of a single artwork which was visible for the entire year of use. After that, calendars used at least six pages, each with a different artwork and a calendar for two consecutive months.

Not only did the Company produce calendars for use in the United States, but for foreign markets as well. Examples from the 1930s and 1940s generally used the indigenous languages, but carried the same artwork as used on American advertising items.

Examples from the 1950s typically portray the language, people, and culture of the country where the calendar was distributed.

1

2

1. Calendar, 1943, 13 x 20 inches. In keeping with the spirit of the time, this six-page calendar shows women in war-related roles. Shown here on the January/February page is a U.S. Army Nurse.

2. Calendar, 1954, 13 x 19⅛ inches. Showing a series of Egyptian movie actresses, this four-page calendar was printed in a combination of both Arabic and French for distribution in the Middle East.

CALENDARS

Starting in the 1960s, smaller business calendars called "calendar displays" were distributed. They consisted of a metal back plate, which carried the advertising for Coca-Cola, and two screw-in posts designed to hold calendar sheets for every day of the year. Once installed, all that needed to be replaced from year to year were the calendar pads. High-quality desk calendars with subtle Coca-Cola advertising were also given to high-volume customers and outstanding employees.

1

2

3

1. Calendar display, 1961, 9⅛ x 12¼ inches. Although the so-called "arciform" logo at the top of this item was not used on any new Coca-Cola advertising after 1963, the durability of a metal calendar display probably would have ensured its use well after that date.

2. Home calendar, 1955, 7 x 6 inches. Because they were generally distributed by bottlers as Christmas gifts, Coca-Cola "home calendars" often showed Santa Claus on the cover page.

3. Desk calendar, 1952, 6¼ inches wide. Changing the plastic date cards provided with this quality bronze desk calendar meant it could be used for any month and year.

SIGNS: *CLOTH SIGNS*

Signs advertising Coca-Cola have been made of a variety of materials and were designed for specific interior and exterior locations.

Signs made of oilcloth (weatherproofed canvas) were among the earliest ones used to advertise Coca-Cola. Such signs were pinned to awnings over the entrances to soda fountains and stores where Coca-Cola was sold. Lighter weight muslin signs were also produced for temporary outdoor locations. Detailed canvas signs were used on Coca-Cola trucks to advertise Company-sponsored radio and television shows in the 1940s and 1950s. Cloth banners, now plastic-coated, are still being used today.

1. Billboard, 1923, 19 feet 8 inches x 8 feet 10 inches. Beginning in 1923, The Coca-Cola Company provided 24-sheet billboards free of charge if the bottlers paid for the advertising space.

2. Canvas sign, c. 1900, 48 x 11 inches. This early canvas sign advertising Coca-Cola in bottles is unusual because it is smaller than most other similar signs from the period, and the trademark has an equal sign instead of a standard hyphen.

SIGNS: PAPER SIGNS

Paper signs advertising Coca-Cola have taken several forms over the years: posters or hangers, window strips, and billboards. Paper posters destined for indoor use were lithographed in full color and usually portrayed young women. Although simply tacked to walls, many also had metal strips on the top and bottom edges and a top-center loop for hanging, and thus were more commonly called hangers.

In 1923, The Coca-Cola Company began creating 24-sheet posters which when assembled produced a billboard measuring approximately twenty-five feet by eleven feet. Of course, once a billboard had been pasted into position, it was irretrievably lost to collectors.

1

1. Paper poster, 1904, 14⅞ x 19⅞ inches. Metropolitan Opera star Lillian Nordica lent her endorsement to Coca-Cola in 1904 and 1905. On the table are a paper-label bottle and a note addressed to "Mme. Nordica." This is a particularly early example of standard advertising that shows the straight-sided bottle for Coca-Cola.

2. Paper window strip, 1949, 24 x 11 inches. The Coca-Cola Company sponsored ventriloquist Edgar Bergen and his dummy Charlie McCarthy on the CBS radio network from 1949 to 1952.

2

SIGNS: CARDBOARD SIGNS

Cardboard is possibly one of the most versatile materials ever used for signs. It can easily be cut to any shape desired, and unlike paper, its rigidity makes it self-supporting so it can be used for various freestanding and hanging displays. Rectangular cardboard signs have been used regularly to advertise Coca-Cola. To guarantee a place on the walls the company introduced corrugated cardboard frames into which standard-sized cardboard signs could be inserted. These were later replaced by frames made of wood and metal finished in a bright metallic gold color. Among the earliest rectangular signs used to advertise Coca-Cola were ones placed in streetcars. These lightweight cardboard signs were placed in a row along the walls on either side of the streetcar's interior immediately below the ceiling line. This form of advertising was considered so important that the Company spent nearly one-sixth of its advertising budget on streetcar signs during the first two decades of the century.

1. Cardboard sign, 1942, in frame, 22¼ x 32¼ inches. War-era advertising didn't ignore women in uniform, as demonstrated by this framed cardboard sign of an Army Nurse stepping off an airplane.

2. Cardboard sign, c.1914, 21 x 10⅞ inches. The Coca-Cola company began warning consumers about low quality imitations. This streetcar sign cautioned people to use the full name for Coca-Cola.

1

2

S I G N S : CUTOUTS

Coca-Cola has been heavily advertised with die-cut cardboard signs. Although thousands of different die-cut signs have been produced over the years, they fall into three main categories: cutouts, festoons, and multipiece displays. Considered to be among the most attractive Coca-Cola collectibles, many die-cut cardboard signs were also embossed or three-dimensional, further adding to their charm.

When used by collectors, the term "cutout" usually refers to a single lithographed piece of die-cut cardboard, either freestanding or hanging. Although many different subjects were used for the artwork, certain general trends are evident: soda fountain customers in the 1910s, bathing beauties in the 1920s, movie stars in the 1930s and military personnel in the 1940s. Starting in the mid-1920s, Coca-Cola with food was also a frequent subject. Beginning in 1931, The Coca-Cola Company began issuing Santa Claus cutouts at Christmas time, a practice that continues to this day.

1. Cardboard cutout, 1935, 33⅛ inches high. Since 1929, the bell-shaped glass, seen here in a large Canadian cardboard cutout, has become the one most closely associated with Coca-Cola worldwide.

2. Cardboard cutout, 1934, 26⅛ inches high. Beginning in 1931 and continuing into the 1960s, artist Haddon Sundblom prepared a different Santa artwork each year, which was then used for magazine ads, posters, and cutouts.

SIGNS

1. Cardboard cutout, 1954, 19 inches high. *Coke Time* with singer Eddie Fisher was a twice-weekly, fifteen-minute musical variety TV program during the 1950s.

2. Cardboard cutout, 1935, 36½ inches high. The Coca-Cola Company frequently employed the services of the foremost illustrators of the day. Norman Rockwell painted the charming artwork that was used for this cutout as well as the 1935 calendar.

3. Cardboard cutout, 1922, 32¼ inches high. This three-fold display shows a young woman in a typical swimsuit of the time riding an "aquaplane," a surfboard-like device towed by a motorboat.

1

2

3

SIGNS

1. Cardboard cutout, 1954, 25⅛ x 34½ inches. The elfin creature shown on this cutout was called "Sprite." Used throughout the 1940s and 1950s, he wore a soda jerk's hat when promoting fountain Coca-Cola, but a bottle cap hat when advertising bottled Coca-Cola.

1

2. Cardboard cutout, 1953, 11⅞ x 14⅛ inches. In the early 1950s, The Coca-Cola Company began to produce special advertising directed toward the African-American market. Famous African-American sports figures and entertainers, such as accordionist Graham Jackson, were recruited to endorse Coca-Cola.

3. Cardboard cutout, 1910, 39½ inches high. Called "Man on the Grass," this cutout is one of the few early examples of advertising for Coca-Cola that show men instead of the more traditional pretty young women.

2

3

S I G N S : FESTOONS

A festoon is a set of die-cut cardboard signs designed to hang as a unit from a wall or soda fountain backbar. Shortly after the turn of the century, the first festoons were nothing more than a series of pieces of die-cut cardboard strung together to spell out the word "Coca-Cola" one letter at a time. Soon festoons became colorful affairs, typically showing attractive women surrounded by a profusion of flowers.

In an attempt to dominate storefront windows, The Coca-Cola Company devised multipiece sets of die-cut cardboard signs capable of spanning an entire window. The use of these displays reached their zenith in the period from the late 1920s through the 1930s, when as many as twenty separate pieces were used to create one display.

1

1. Cardboard festoon, 1929, 8 feet wide. Because they were made of several individual pieces of cardboard, later festoons could be adapted to the space available. The "Orchid Festoon" shown here used multicolored satin ribbons to connect the pieces.

2. Cardboard festoon, c. 1910, 57 inches wide. The earliest festoons for Coca-Cola were made of several pieces of die-cut cardboard fastened together with grommets. When it was tacked to the backbar, the end pieces hung down naturally under their own weight.

2

SIGNS: METAL SIGNS

Although most metal signs were designed exclusively for outdoor use because of their durability, some were elaborately designed and intended specifically for indoor use.

Some outdoor signs were made of thin tin-plated metal with a lithographed finish, while others meant for extended use were made of heavy metal with a porcelain enamel finish. The thin metal signs usually had no holes for hanging and were called tacker signs because they were installed by nailing right through the metal to attach them. Porcelain signs came with pre-drilled holes, grommets, or brackets for hanging. Starting in the 1920s, signs were designed with special frames and poles so that they could stand alone outside outlets. Two-sided flange signs were also made which were attached to buildings at right angles.

Indoor metal signs were generally smaller than their outdoor counterparts. Many were lithographed in full color to enhance the advertising, as well as the interior of the store as well.

1. Metal sign, c. 1903, 8⅝ x 10¾ inches. This oval sign may be the first metal sign to feature the straight-sided, paper-label bottle for Coca-Cola.

2. Metal sign, 1954, 19 inches wide. Twelve-bottle cartons, such as the one shown on this die-cut sign, were used on an experimental basis by some bottlers in the mid-1950s.

SIGNS

1

1. Metal sign, 1933, 27 x 19 inches. The bottle on this sign is commonly called the Christmas bottle because of the December 25, 1923, patent date on the bottle.

2. Metal sign, c. 1910, 35½ x 11⅜ inches. The paper-label bottle was used not just in the United States, but throughout the rest of the world as well, as evidenced by this French language tacker sign.

2

3. Metal sign, 1927, 30 x 7¼ inches. This two-sided arrow sign originally hung from a wrought-iron bracket fastened at right angles to a wall.

3

SIGNS

1. Metal sign, 1927, 11⅛ x 8⅛ inches. This small sign is a rare example of the Coca-Cola trademark being partially obscured in the artwork.

2. Metal sign, 1970, 15⅝ x 21⅞ inches. Made in Mexico, this self-framed sign with photograph artwork shows that pretty girls could still sell Coca-Cola in the 1970s.

SIGNS

Glass signs with Coca-Cola advertising first appeared around 1900. The earliest known examples are oval or round and carry the "Drink Coca-Cola 5¢" message with no pictorial graphics. They were ordinarily hung by attached metal chains. In the 1920s, round glass signs were designed to be glued directly to mirrored walls and backbars in drug stores and soda fountains. In the 1930s, Art Deco reverse-painted glass signs were available for upscale locations. The use of this type of glass sign ended by the 1950s, replaced by self-contained electric light-up fixtures with glass panels.

1. Glass sign, 1933, 28¼ x 11¼ inches. With its wooden embellishments, this black and silver reverse-painted glass sign epitomizes the Art Deco style.

2. Plastic sign, c. 1962, 13¼ x 9¼ inches. Unlike earlier signs that were constructed from several materials, many modern signs are made from molded plastic to achieve the same three-dimensional effect.

SIGNS: WOODEN SIGNS

Beginning in 1933 and continuing into the 1950s, the Company used mass-produced wooden signs for indoor use. Most of these signs were not made exclusively of wood, but had three-dimensional embellishments made of other materials including metal, plaster, rope, cloth, and plastic.

Fiberboard was temporarily used for outdoor signs during World War II. There are a number of instances where the artwork used on fiberboard signs was the same as that previously used on metal signs.

1

2

1. Wood and metal sign, 1937, 23½ x 23 inches. Made of plywood with applied three-dimensional metal trim.

2. Wooden menu sign, 1940, 13¾ x 27¼ inches. With its low prices and unusual food choices, this artifact gives insight into a typical luncheonette menu of the 1940s.

S I G N S : Special use Signs

The advertising for Coca-Cola served a secondary purpose on some signs. The primary purpose was utilitarian. Thermometers, menu boards, chalkboards, "Push" and "Pull" door signs, and door push bars are examples of such signs.

1. Wooden thermometer, c. 1920, 5⅛ x 20⅞ inches. Because of its usefulness, this thermometer would have remained in place long after other advertising items had been discarded.

2. Metal thermometer, 1941, 6⅞ x 15¾ inches. With its Art Deco design, this thermometer would have complemented the design of up-to-date drug stores and soda fountains in the 1940s.

3. Metal chalkboard, 1940, 19¼ x 27 inches. Chalkboards with Coca-Cola advertising have been distributed to food retailers since the 1920s. The artwork in the lower right corner of this one is called the "Silhouette Girl" logo.

1

2

3

LIGHTING AND LIGHTED SIGNS

The earliest known lighting fixtures to advertise Coca-Cola were made of leaded or mosaic glass. Rectangular in shape, these fixtures were intended to hang over a soda fountain or in a window display.

The next lighting fixtures to advertise Coca-Cola were spherical. There are two versions of the leaded glass "ball" shade: one designed to hang from the ceiling and the other to sit atop dispensing units. These lights have been reproduced in small quantities, but without the curved glass of the originals.

The 1920s saw the traditional-shaped leaded glass shade, equipped with a chain for hanging. Since this fixture was issued for a number of years, there are several variations, including more recent reproductions.

1

1. Leaded glass chandelier, 1911, 25½ inches long. This particular one-of-a-kind rectangular light remained hanging in the same store for over fifty years.

2. Leaded glass light, c. 1920, 36 inches high. Made by the Metropolitan Art Glass Company of New York, this illuminated bottle was used both indoors and out to advertise Coca-Cola.

3. Glass lighted sign, c. 1938, 13½ inches high. The bottle shown on this lighted counter sign carries the design patent number assigned to the shape of the hobbleskirt bottle in 1937.

2

3

LIGHTING AND LIGHTED SIGNS

Another leaded glass item introduced in the 1920s was a three-foot high replica of the hobbleskirt bottle. By the mid-1920s, milk-glass shades began to replace leaded glass fixtures. Made of a single piece of molded glass, the first of these shades had Coca-Cola printed in red along with green pinstriping. A Brass tassel hanging from the bottom and a brass fitter attached to the top completed the unit. Less ornate milk-glass shades were used throughout the 1930s, and unlike other decorative lights these were truly meant to light an area.

1. Milk-glass light with metal tassel, c. 1929, 13½-inch diameter. These lights cost $8 each from the Progress Gas Fixture Company of New York, and were used in soda fountains and bottling plants.

1

LIGHTING AND LIGHTED SIGNS

While early lighted signs were made of glass, most examples since the 1960s have been made of plastic. Most lighted signs were illuminated by ordinary incandescent or fluorescent light bulbs. Neon tubing was also used to light some signs and clocks as early as the 1930s. Some examples even had the neon tubing bent into the shape of the Coca-Cola trademark.

1

2

1. Metal and plastic lighted sign, c. 1950, 15½ x 15½ inches. Signs such as this one were used to remind customers to place their empty bottles in the rack next to the vending machine.

2. Neon sign, 1988, 19¾ x 17¼ inches. This neon sign was used by the Coca-Cola bottler in Philadelphia, home of the Liberty Bell.

CLOCKS

Clocks comprise one of the more expensive but enduring forms of advertising used for Coca-Cola. The first clocks were made by the Baird Clock Company of Platsburgh, New York. Initially used in 1893, they cost the Company $2.75 each and were given as premiums to dealers who bought fifty gallons of Coca-Cola syrup in a year. Baird clocks, key-wound and pendulum-driven, had large round faces with Roman numerals. They had two round doors – one over the face and the other over the pendulum.

Next came the schoolhouse clock. The upper portion was octagonal in shape and made of finished wood surrounding a glass-covered, circular face. The lower portion consisted of a wood and glass door covering a compartment for the pendulum.

1

2

1. Pendulum clock, c. 1895, 31 inches high. This particular example of a "figure-eight" Baird clock does not appear to have been refinished as was the custom for such composition clocks when they started to show signs of wear.

2. Pendulum clock, c. 1900, 26 inches high. Many of these ornate schoolhouse clocks, such as this one made by the Welch Manufacturing Company, still work today.

CLOCKS

In about 1905, The Coca-Cola Company began distributing large rectangular clocks, commonly called regulator clocks. This type of clock had a wooden case with a single door consisting of two framed pieces of glass. The face carried the advertising for Coca-Cola printed in red and used the same face as on the earlier schoolhouse clock. This kind of clock was produced from 1910 through to 1941 with variations in design and advertising message.

1. Electric clock, 1940, 18¼ x 18¼ inches. Besides drawing attention to the clock itself, the neon tubing surrounding the face was intended to help illuminate the store's interior at night.

2. Pendulum clock, 1911, 39½ inches high. Because the woman portrayed on the lower panel is reminiscent of the artwork of illustrator Charles Dana Gibson, this Gilbert clock is commonly called the "Gibson Girl" clock.

3. Electric clock, 1948, 36 inches wide. This deluxe clock with ornamental rings and background panel was intended for high-quality establishments.

2

1

3

CLOCKS

Electric clocks advertising Coca-Cola began to appear in the early 1930s. The advertising usually appeared either on the face of the clock or on the glass covering the face. At first the cases were made of wood and metal. Plastic cases and faces began to appear in the late 1950s. There are many styles and variations of clocks, made by dozens of manufacturers. The slogans and graphics, materials, and design, help collectors date these myriad clocks.

In addition, the Company and its local bottlers also distributed table and desk clocks. Among the earliest of these, dating from around 1910, are clocks with leather-covered cases with the advertising appearing in gold-stamped lettering.

1. Electric clock, c. 1963, 16 x 16 inches. With its all-plastic case illuminated from inside by a ring-shaped florescent bulb, this clock carries the popular "things go better with Coke" logo.

2. Wind-up clock, c. 1910, 3⅛ x 3⅛ inches. Decorated with gold-leaf lettering, leather desk clocks such as the one shown here were distributed from 1905 to 1915.

TOYS AND GAMES

For some collectors, toys and games are the most beloved Coca-Cola collectibles. Until the Company instituted a licensing program in the 1980s, toy manufacturers in many countries produced countless toys with the Coca-Cola trademark, but without the Company's involvement. However, the Company did produce such things as playing cards and games to promote the sale of Coca-Cola.

Bottlers who needed a way to encourage the return of empty bottles or increase sales devised a coupon scheme. After amassing a sufficient number of coupons, the customer could then visit the bottler and exchange the coupons for useful "gifts." Among the most popular of these premiums were mass-produced toys to which the bottlers simply added the Coca-Cola logo.

1. Cardboard airplane, c. 1928, 10 inches long. Coca-Cola celebrated Charles Lindbergh's 1927 trans-Atlantic flight with the distribution of this replica glider of his "Spirit of St. Louis" plane.

2. Cardboard whistle, c. 1910, 1¼ x 6¼ inches. Featuring the straight-sided, paper-label bottle, this whistle produces a high-pitched, kazoo-like sound when blown.

TOYS AND GAMES

Toys and games form such an eclectic group of objects that it is difficult to generalize about them. Since most of toys were produced without the knowledge or permission of The Coca-Cola Company, there is little information about exactly what was produced and when. For this reason, perhaps no other area of Coca-Cola collecting is as exciting as this one, since previously unknown toys are constantly being discovered.

1

1. Metal truck, 1931, 11 inches long. This immensely popular, miniature A-frame Coca-Cola truck was sold in department stores and mail-order catalogs at a cost of about 50¢ each.

2. Metal train, c. 1930, 30 inches long. This key-wound American Flyer train was probably ordered by the St. Louis, Missouri, bottler to be used as a premium.

3. Boxed game, 1949, 9¼ x 3¼ x 1¼ inches. The object of this "Tower of Hannoi" game was to move the eight circular disks from one peg to another by following a set of rules.

2

3

TOYS AND GAMES

Another category of items frequently thought of as toys are miniatures, small-sized replicas of larger items. For Coca-Cola, miniatures included bottles, cartons, cases, coolers, dispensers, and glasses. It was not surprising that The Coca-Cola Company distributed miniature versions of its own merchandising items, thereby enabling children to play at being Coca-Cola customers and dealers. Toy manufacturers have also made toy coolers and dispensers, some of which double as savings banks.

1. Plastic cooler, c. 1950, 5⅛ x 4 x 5⅛ inches. This miniature picnic cooler came complete with clear plastic ice and two plastic Coca-Cola bottles.

2a and **2b** Plastic bank, c. 1948, 5⅛ inches high. A miniature replica of a Vendo V-83 machine, this toy bank dispensed a miniature Coca-Cola bottle when a coin was inserted.

3. Plastic truck, 1949, 11 inches long. This toy truck, made by Louis Marx & Co. of New York, is a fairly faithful representation of the gull-wing trucks used by many Coca-Cola bottlers.

TOYS AND GAMES

Coca-Cola bottlers have always distributed playing cards. In the 1930s and 1940s, the Company and its bottlers took advantage of the card-playing craze by distributing numerous decks of playing cards advertising Coca-Cola. Distributing Coca-Cola playing cards has been a standard advertising practice since that time. While collectors prefer complete decks in original boxes, there are decks so difficult to obtain in this form that some collectors have settled for single playing cards.

1. Playing cards, c. 1940, 2¼ x 3½ inches. Made by the Atlantic Playing Card Company, these cards show the familiar "Silhouette Girl" logo.

2. Playing cards, 1915, 2½ x 3½ inches. These cards, showing the "Elaine" artwork from the 1915 Coca-Cola calendar, could be ordered from the Western Coca-Cola Bottling Company for 25¢.

EDUCATIONAL MATERIALS

When Coca-Cola was first sold, its tonic properties were advertised as being perfect for the work-weary. Because of the high caffeine content (which was nearly three times what it is now), combined with erroneous rumors about alcohol and cocaine, some mothers forbade their children to drink it. For its part, The Coca-Cola Company did not try to appeal to children in its early years. With the passage of the Pure Food and Drug Act in 1906 and the reduction of the caffeine content in the late 1910s, The Coca-Cola Company began a slow and subtle foray into the so-called youth market in the 1920s.

The Coca-Cola Company used the educational system to reach children. Educators were sent free booklets telling them how safe and wholesome Coca-Cola was. Many bottlers donated utilitarian items to schools. Coca-Cola pencils, blotters, clocks, and calendars, all very obviously useful, were the most popular giveaways.

1

1. Booklet, 1928, 7½ x 5¼ inches. To help children learn the alphabet, each page of this full-color "ABC Booklet" has a poem about a letter of the alphabet.

2. Blotter, c. 1935, 3⅞ x 9 inches. This Canadian blotter provided healthful hints and could also be used as a ruler.

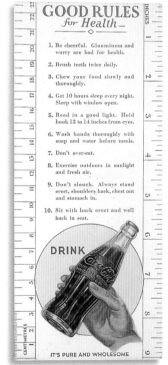

2

EDUCATIONAL MATERIALS

In 1923 it was proposed that bottlers "give each child a ruler, a pencil and three blotters." It was predicted that if a bottler carried out this program for three years at a cost of $600, he would have 5,000 new customers. Although pencils and blotters had long been standard Coca-Cola giveaways, rulers were another matter. The Company began producing a special ruler imprinted with the words, "Do Unto Others As You Would Have Them Do Unto You." This Golden Rule ruler, as it was called, had possibly the longest life of any advertising item for Coca-Cola – it remained virtually unchanged for more than forty-five years.

1. School kit in envelope, 1935, 9 x 11⅞ inches. For 10¢, a schoolchild received a bottle of Coca-Cola along with a writing tablet, a pencil, a blotter, and a ruler.

2. Mechanical pencil, 1942, 5⅞ inches long. The miniature bottle on the end of this mechanical lead pencil is actually filled with Coca-Cola.

1

2

EDUCATIONAL MATERIALS

Because they were given out in such large quantities, educational items are readily available for today's collectors. Additionally, since the same kinds of items were distributed over several decades, it is sometimes difficult to date them correctly. The advertising slogans printed on these items can frequently be used to pinpoint the years of use more accurately.

1

1. Cardboard map, c. 1955, 24 x 18½ inches. With its distances between major U.S. cities, this wall map could have been used in schools as well as service stations.

NOVELTIES

One of the most popular, personal, and inexpensive forms of advertising has been novelties, small useful items that consumers of Coca-Cola would invariably carry with them. Each item cost mere pennies, so that number of such items distributed is staggering.

Leather novelties included wallets, coin purses, match safes, and pocket notebooks. The advertising on the leather was usually imprinted using gold leaf. Wallets and coin purposes were issued from early in the century to the present time.

The use of book matches to advertise Coca-Cola began shortly after the turn of the century. The few that have survived testify to the wide variety of cover designs that were used in the early years. Girls, straight-sided bottles, and diamond-shaped bottle labels were the most common subjects. In addition to the advertising on the cover, it was not unusual for early matchbooks to have advertising slogans on each individual match.

1a

1b

2

3

1a and 1b Match books, c. 1912, 1⅜ x 2⅛ inches each. This pair of match books exemplifies how the same artwork was adapted for both bottle and fountain sales.

2. Leather coin purse, c. 1910, 2½ x 2¼ inches. With gold-leaf stamping, more expensive novelties such as this one were generally given to store clerks in order to build product loyalty.

3. Leather match safe, 1906, 1¼ x 2⅛ inches. The Coca-Cola Company often took part in trade conventions such as those held by the National Association of Retail Druggists (NARD).

NOVELTIES

Made of celluloid or metal, or a combination of both, a watch fob was attached by a leather strap to a pocket watch. Although there are many different examples of watch fobs advertising Coca-Cola, they were used for a short period beginning about 1905.

Perhaps the most enduring novelty of all, bottle openers were virtually indestructible. Usually stamped from a flat sheet of metal, they were easily and cheaply produced. Because individual bottlers usually arranged for the manufacture of openers, there are countless different examples available to collectors.

1. Metal watch fob, c. 1910, 1⅜ x 1½ inches. Between 1908 and 1912, the swastika was recognized the world over as a good-luck symbol.

2a, 2b, 2c, and **2d** Metal openers, c. 1905 to c. 1925, 2¼ to 7¼ inches long. As seen in this photograph, bottle openers were produced in a variety of shapes and sizes.

1

2a

2b

2c

2d

NOVELTIES

Celluloid-covered items advertising Coca-Cola included signs, pocket mirrors, watch fobs, and cuff links, while items made entirely of celluloid included bookmarks, pocketknife handles, and covers for pocket notebooks, stamp holders and blotter pads.

From the late 1890s and well into the 1910s, the Company used 'Japanese' rice paper fans with bamboo handles. After that time, cardboard fans were distributed. Fans were given away to individuals, as well as to churches and other civic organizations.

1

2

1. Rice paper fan, c. 1900, 10 x 15 inches. Although the construction of this fan is typical of those from the early 1900s, the artwork on this example with its spider, web, dragonfly, and other insects is quite unusual.

2. Pocket mirror, 1914, 1¾ x 2¾ inches. The artwork on Company-issued pocket mirrors was usually the same as that on the annual Coca-Cola calendar and other items. This mirror is unusual in that the only other item to carry the same artwork is a 1914 magazine ad.

3. Key and ring, 1959, 4½ inches long. In a clever pun the key says, "Steady promotion is the key to sales."

3

NOVELTIES

In addition to the novelties already mentioned, ice picks, fly swatters, key rings, thimbles, salt and pepper shakers, cigarette lighters, mechanical pencils, pens, ashtrays, scorekeepers, sheet music, jewelry, advertising buttons, and sewing kits have all been used to promote Coca-Cola.

1. Metal pocket lighter, c. 1955, 2⅛ x 1¼ inches. The Coca-Cola Company occasionally distributed novelties with "Drink Coca-Cola" in many languages.

2. Table lighter, c. 1960, 4¼ inches high. This attractive lighter seems to be saying, "Have a Coke and a smoke."

3. Metal spinner, c. 1900, 2¼ inches long. When friends gathered around a soda fountain table, they could use this hand-shaped, lithographed tin spinner to determine who paid next.

MISCELLANEOUS ITEMS

For a variety of reasons, there are Coca-Cola collectibles that don't fit conveniently into any of the previous chapters. For example, stationery, invoices, receipts, and checks are used in normal everyday business operations. When such items carry the Coca-Cola trademark, they become instantly collectible. Similarly, The Coca-Cola Company presented plaques and awards to its employees and bottlers.

Ordinary building hardware, such as doorknobs and padlocks, when used in Coca-Cola office buildings and plants, was sometimes marked with the Coca-Cola logo. Today the disposable plastic seals on syrup containers are similarly marked. Although these items would ordinarily go unnoticed, the inclusion of the Coca-Cola trademark renders them collectible.

1. Metal doorknobs, c. 1915, 2⅛-inch diameter. When The Coca-Cola Company built branch offices, they equipped them with brass door knobs. This one is from the Candler Building in Baltimore, Maryland.

2. Plaque, 1953, 18 x 7¼ inches. The bottler in Newcastle, Indiana, was presented with this "per capita" award for selling 200 bottles of Coca-Cola to each man, woman, and child in his territory in the year 1953.

MISCELLANEOUS ITEMS

1

2

1. Bakelite radio, 1933, 23¼ inches high. At a cost of $18.75 each, the "Bottle Radio" was one of the most expensive advertising items presented to retailers during the Great Depression.

2. Electric toaster, c. 1930, 7¼-inch diameter. After they had been made, sandwiches were put into this appliance in order to toast the Coca-Cola trademark onto the bread.

3. Wooden bench, c. 1920, 47½ inches.

3

MISCELLANEOUS ITEMS

Over the years, in an effort to increase their own business, manufacturers of advertising items have presented the Company and its bottlers with new ideas for promoting Coca-Cola. This group of short-lived items includes some of the most desirable of all Coca-Cola collectibles.

The Coca-Cola trademark has been used by other firms to advertise their own products. Many manufacturers of advertising material have used Coca-Cola items made by them as exemplars of the quality of their work.

1. Plastic mileage meter, c. 1950, 7 inches high. By spinning the drum inside this mileage meter, a motorist could determine how far it was from Martinsville, Virginia, to other places.

2. Wall planters, 1932, each 12 inches high. This planter set was designed for upscale outlets.

3. Cardboard coaster, c. 1940, 3⅛-inch diameter. This coaster is an example of advertising items distributed by manufacturers of merchandising items that advertise not only their products, but Coca-Cola as well.

REPRODUCTION, FANTASY, AND . . .

The 1970s saw The Coca-Cola Company's first real interest in the memorabilia craze that had begun sweeping the nation. The Company offered reproductions to a nostalgia-hungry public.

Technically speaking, a reproduction is a copy of an older item. At first glance, the casual observer may not notice any discernible difference between the two.

A fantasy item is one that appears to be old, but in reality is not. Unlike a reproduction, a fantasy item has no original counterpart. To give them an air of authenticity, most fantasy items incorporate old artwork and slogans as part of their design.

In the mid-1980s, The Coca-Cola Company established a licensing program whereby they officially sanctioned the manufacture of items bearing the Coca-Cola trademark.

2a

1

2b

1. Cardboard sign, 1973, 18⅛ x 23 inches. Shown here is the advertising used by The Coca-Cola Company for the first set of three reproduction trays that were offered for sale in the United States in 1973.

2a and **2b** Tray, 1923, 10⅜ x 13¼ inches, and reproduction 1974, 12⅜ x 15⅛ inches. Even though the Company used a different shape from the original (above), the reproduction tray (below) is still mistaken today for an old tray.

. . . *LICENSED ITEMS*

1

2

3

1. Fantasy belt buckle, c. 1973, 4 x 2⅝ inches. Belt buckles, such as this one made of brass and marked "Tiffany ," first appeared in collectors' markets in the early 1970s.

2. Fantasy pocketknife, c. 1975, 2½ inches long. Easily mass-produced by unscrupulous individuals, fantasy pocketknives can be found at almost any flea market.

3. Fantasy pocket watch and fob, c. 1972, 7½ inches long. This pocket watch is authentically old, but the new face was added in more recent times. The attached silver watch fob and leather strap are entirely new.

4a, 4b, and **4c** Commemorative bottles, 1975, 1986, and 1993, 7¼ inches, 9¼ inches, and 7¼ inches high. Bottles commemorating special events and celebrities are a popular sub-category for many of today's collectors.

4a

4b

4c

FURTHER READING

BOOKS ABOUT COCA-COLA COLLECTIBLES

Biasio, Mariateresa & Fadini, Ugo, *Coca-Cola un mito.* Rome: Leonardo De Luca, 1992. (110 pages)

Cholot, Gerard, Cuzon-Verrier, Daniel, & Lemare, Pierre, *Les Plus Belles Affiches de Coca-Cola.* Paris: Editions Denoël, 1986. (144 pages)

Cope, Jim, *Soda Water Advertising.* Orange, TX: author, 1971. (80 pages)

de Courtivron, Gael, *Collectible Coca-Cola Toy Trucks.* Paducah, KY: Collector Books, 1995. (240 pages)

Ebner, Steve & Wright, Jeff, *Vintage Coca-Cola Machines.* Gaithersburg, MD: Fun-tronics, 1989. (110 pages)

Goldstein, Shelley & Helen, *Coca-Cola Collectibles, Vols. 1–4.* Woodland Hills, CA: authors, 1972–76. (78–88 pages each)

Hill, Deborah Goldstein, *Price Guide to Coca-Cola Collectibles.* Radnor, PA: Wallace-Homestead, 1991. (196 pages)

Mix, Richard, *The Mix Guide to Commemorative Bottles.* San Antonio, TX: Multi-Ads, 1990. (200 pages)

Munsey, Cech, *The Illustrated Guide to the Collectibles of Coca-Cola.* New York: Hawthorn Books, Inc., 1972. (334 pages)

Murken-Altrogge, Christa, *Coca-Cola Art: Konsum, Kult, Kunst.* München: Klinkhardt & Biermann, 1991. (208 pages)

Petretti, Allan, *Petretti's Coca-Cola Collectibles Price Guide, 9th Edition.* Hackensack, NJ: Nostalgia Publications, Inc., 1994. (500 pages)

Schmidt, Bill & Jan, *The Schmidt Museum Collection of Coca-Cola Memorabilia.* Elizabethtown, KY: Schmidt Books, 1983. (160 pages)

Weinberger, Marty & Don, *Coca-Cola Trays from Mexico & Canada.* Willow Grove, PA: authors, 1979. (40 pages)

Wilson, Al & Helen, *Wilson's Coca-Cola Price Guide.* Atglen, PA: Schiffer Publishing, 1994. (256 pages)

BOOKS ABOUT THE HISTORY OF COCA-COLA

Allen, Frederick, *Secret Formula: How Brilliant Marketing and Relentless Salesmanship Made Coca-Cola the Best Known Product in the World.* New York: HarperBusiness, 1994. (500 pages)

Candler, Charles Howard, *Asa Griggs Candler.* Atlanta: Emory University, 1950. (502 pages)

Coca-Cola Company, *The Coca-Cola Company: An Illustrated Profile.* Atlanta: author, 1974. (110 pages)

Dietz, Lawrence, *Soda Pop.* New York: Simon & Schuster, 1973. (184 pages)

Elliott, Charles, *"Mr. Anonymous" Robert Woodruff of Coca-Cola.* Atlanta: Cherokee Publishing Company, 1982. (310 pages)

Graham, Elizabeth Candler, *The Real Ones, Four Generations of the First Family of Coca-Cola.* Fort Lee, NJ: Barricade Books, 1992. (344 pages)

Hoy, Anne, *Coca-Cola: The First 100 Years.* Atlanta: The Coca-Cola Company, 1986. (160 pages)

Kahn, E.J., *The Big Drink: The Story of Coca-Cola.* New York: Random House, 1960. (174 pages)

Louis, J.C., & Yazijian, Harvey, *The Cola Wars.* New York: Everest House, 1980. (386 pages)

Mayo, P. Randolph, *Coca-Cola Heritage: A Photographic History of the Biedenharn Coca-Cola Bottling Business.* San Antonio, TX: author, 1990 (118 pages)

Oliver, Thomas, *The Real Coke, The Real Story.* New York: Random House, 1986. (234 pages)

Patou-Senez, Julie, *Coca-Cola Story.* Paris: G. Authier, 1978. (274 pages)

Pendergrast, Mark, *For God, Country, and Coca-Cola.* New York: Scribner's, 1993. (556 pages)

Shartar, Martin & Shavin, Norman, *The Wonderful World of Coca-Cola.* Atlanta: Capricorn Corporation, 1981. (64 pages)

Staples, Bob & Charles, Barbara, *Dream of Santa: Haddon Sundblom's Vision.* Washington, DC: Staples & Charles, 1992. (84 pages)

Steinbach Palazzini, Fiora, *Coca-Cola Superstar.* New York: Barron's, 1989. (142 pages)

Watters, Pat, *Coca-Cola: An Illustrated History.* Garden City, NY: Doubleday & Co., Inc., 1978. (288 pages)

USEFUL ADDRESSES

C. C. Tray-ders, 611 North 5th St., Reading, PA 19601–2201, USA. Appraisers.

Coca-Cola Collectors Club, P.O. Box 49166, Atlanta, GA 30359–1166, USA. International organization.

Coca-Cola Fifth Avenue, 711 Fifth Avenue, New York, NY 10022, USA. Coca-Cola display and store.

Memorabilia Club, Casella postale 540, 20101, Italy. Italian organization.

Muddy River Trading Company, 4803 Lange Lane, SW, Roanoke, VA 24018, USA. Auctions.

Nostalgia Publications, 21 South Lake Dr., Hackensack, NJ 07601, USA. Auctions.

Pop's Mail Order Collectibles, 4439 Hudgins, Memphis, TN 38116, USA. Catalog sales.

Schmidt Museum of Coca-Cola Memorabilia, 1201 North Dixie, Elizabethtown, KY 42702, USA. Museum and store.

Tucker Bay Company, P.O. Box 70127, Stockton, CA 95267, USA. Auctions.

U-Grade It Video Auctions, 4411 Bazetta Road, Cortland, Ohio 44410, USA. Auctions.

The World of Coca-Cola, 55 Martin Luther King, Jr., Drive, Atlanta, GA 30303, USA. Museum and store.

> The authors, Bill Bateman & Randy Schaeffer, look forward to hearing from fellow Coca-Cola collectors and enthusiasts. They can be reached by mail at 611 North 5th Street, Reading, PA 19601, by phone at (610) 373–3333, or by e-mail: bateman@kutztown.edu. They are also interested in adding old and unusual items to their collection.

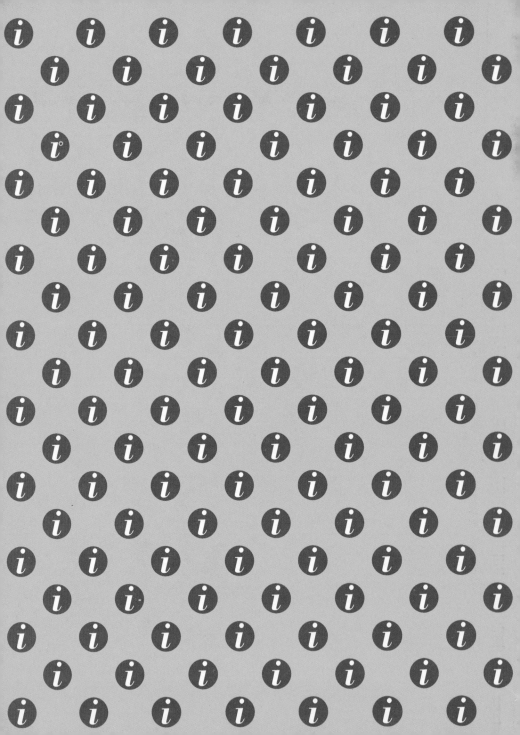